HOW TO LOOK AFTER

PET DOG

A PRACTICAL GUIDE TO CARING FOR YOUR PET, IN STEP-BY-STEP PHOTOGRAPHS

DAVID ALDERTON

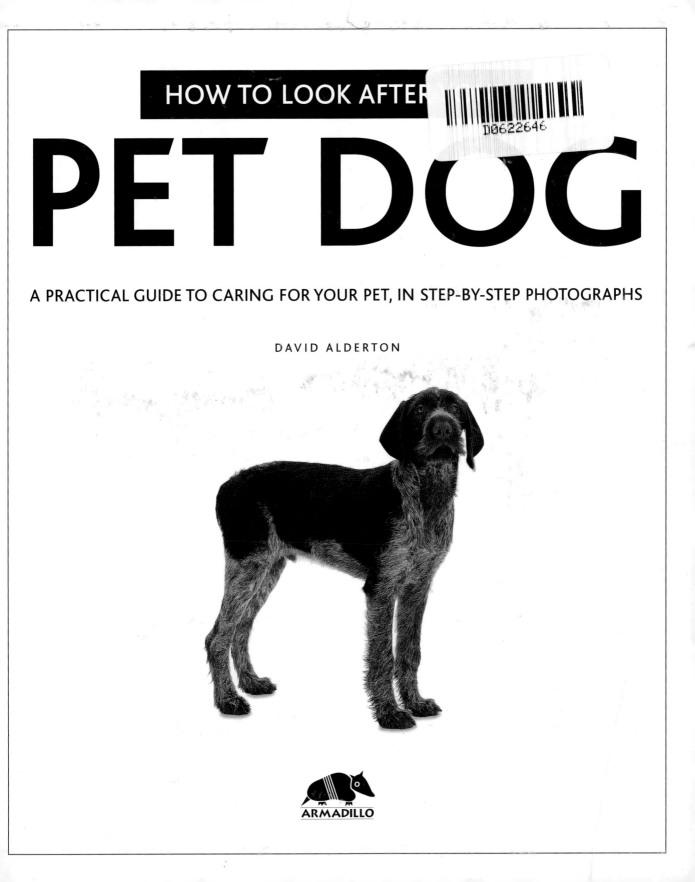

D062646

ARMADILLO

Introduction

It's really important that dogs have plenty of attention and are made to feel like members of the family. At first, you will also need to be prepared to spend time training your pet, especially if you start out with a puppy. Dogs are active by nature, and they need to go for a walk at least once a day. Depending on the type of dog that you choose, you may also have to groom your pet every day.

Remember too that larger dogs have bigger appetites, and so are more expensive to keep than smaller ones. Hopefully your pet will stay healthy, but vaccines and deworming tablets will be necessary, so there will be some veterinary costs. Most dogs today live for more than 10 years, with smaller dogs often living into their teens.

Your dog needs to be fed either once or twice a day, at around the same time each day.

You can share the care of your dog with a brother or a sister.

Dogs as part of the family

It is a good thing if everyone in your family is as enthusiastic as you are about choosing a dog as a pet. Dogs get on well with people, being friendly by nature, but they can soon tell if someone dislikes them.

As far as other pets are concerned, a dog may try to chase a cat at first, but soon learns not to do so, after a cat turns and hisses at it. Always be sure to keep your dog away from small pets such as rabbits, however, because they are a dog's natural prey and will probably become distressed by being near them.

Space and boredom

Dogs do not settle well in apartments – they need a home with a garden in most cases. You also need to ensure that your pet does not become bored when you are out at school and your parents are at work. Dogs, especially puppies, may become destructive around the home if they are left alone for a long time every day. Give your pet plenty of exercise and lots of toys to prevent this happening when you are away from home.

Your dog will need lots of exercise to keep it fit and happy.

Choosing the right pet for you

While many pet dogs belong to particular breeds, others may be bred from matings between two breeds or may even be of no particular breed. It is important to know approximately how big your puppy will be when it is older and it's much easier to know how tall pure-bred puppies will grow, but in other cases, look at their feet. Those dogs that have relatively large feet compared with their body size at a young age are likely to grow into big dogs.

Dogs that have parents and grandparents of different breeds are called mutts.

Pure-bred puppies may look very similar, especially if they are from the same litter.

What is a dog?

Dogs are mammals, and they can remain warm even if their surroundings are much colder, partly because of the hair on their bodies. Female dogs, called bitches, give birth to young puppies that are then suckled on milk, like other mammals.

All domestic dogs are descended from the grey wolf, which used to be found across the northern part of the world. No one is sure when grey wolves began to develop into dogs – probably 10,000–100,000 years ago. To begin with, orphaned wolf cubs were reared as pets and so became tame. Such wolves could help people hunt for food and warn them of danger, especially at night, thanks to their keen hearing. Over the centuries, such wolves bred and slowly changed into dogs.

The ancestor of all domestic dogs is the grey wolf.

Coats

Some breeds of dog have short, smooth coats that lie close to their body. Others have much longer fur, or fur with a wiry texture. All three coat types occur in Dachshunds. There are even some dogs that have very little hair on their bodies, such as the Chinese crested.

Size

Dog breeds today vary in size from the tiny Chihuahua, which stands no taller than an adult hand, to giants of the group such as the Irish wolfhound, which may measure 90cm (35in) in height at the shoulder. A great range in size can also be seen in the grey wolf population.

Chihuahuas are tiny dogs and can have short or long coats

The Irish wolfhound is a huge dog – it stands as tall as a young child.

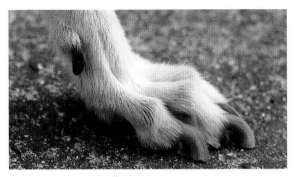

The "dew claw" is sometimes removed to keep the dog from getting tangled up in undergrowth.

Ears and noses

Some dogs have ears that are upright, like wolves do, which help them to hear sounds clearly. Others have ears that hang down – this protects them from injury when they run through undergrowth. Dogs with broad noses have a keen sense of smell.

Teeth and claws

As hunters, all dogs have sharp teeth, and those at the corners of the mouth are long and pointed. These are called the canines. Dogs have claws on their toes that are very broad and help them to run fast without slipping over. So-called "dew claws" are often present some distance up on the inside of each leg. They are often removed early in a dog's life, because dogs can get caught up by them, which is very painful.

Dogs are hunters, which is why they have sharp, pointed teeth, large ears and a strong sense of smell.

Tails

Dogs use their tails to keep in touch with each other. A dog that is happy to see you will run forwards, wagging its tail as it goes – but if it is frightened or upset, then it will keep its tail down between its legs. When a dog is swimming, it uses its tail like a ship's rudder as it steers through the water.

Long ears protect a dog's hearing.

Broad nose gives good sense of smell.

Dogs have many of the same features as their ancestor, the grey wolf.

Claws help a dog to grip the ground when it runs.

The tail shows how a dog is feeling and helps to guide it in water.

Dog breeds

One of the easiest ways to identify a breed is the shape of the face. Some dogs have very pointed faces, but others have much more rounded faces, such as boxers. Their ears can differ in appearance too – they are raised in breeds such as the German shepherd, and hang down the sides of the face in the case of many hounds. Some dogs occur in more than one size. For instance, there are standard, miniature and toy varieties of the poodle, all of which can be bred in a wide range of colours, from white to apricot and chocolate to black.

The Chinese Crested "powder puff" has fluffy fur.

Chinese crested dog

This breed occurs in two very different forms. The "powder puff" form looks like an ordinary dog, but there is a hairless form that has a bald body, with individual markings. It still has traces of fur on its head, feet and tail. Both types of Chinese crested may be present in the same litter of puppies.

Originally bred to tackle wolves, the Irish wolfhound is a friendly dog.

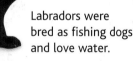

Labradors were bred as fishing dogs and love water.

Labradors

The Labrador retriever is probably the most popular breed of dog in the world today. It has been bred in three different colours, of which yellow and black are most common, with the chocolate variety being more rare. Its ancestors used to work with fishermen, and helped them to pull in their nets.

Irish wolfhound

Most dog breeds were originally kept as working dogs. The Irish wolfhound was bred to tackle large, aggressive wolves in its native Ireland. When they became extinct, the breed itself almost died out too. Luckily it was saved, and these lively, friendly hounds still rank among the giants of today's dog world.

Shar pei

This is a breed that almost became extinct in the 1980s. It is an ancient Chinese dog that was originally kept for fighting, and it is very unusual because it has a bluish rather than a pink tongue, wrinkly skin and a frowning expression. Dog lovers around the world helped to ensure its survival, and these dogs are very often seen at top shows today.

The Shar pei is a Chinese dog, originally kept for fighting.

Chihuahuas

Originating from the region of Mexico after which it is named, the Chihuahua has been bred in both different colours and patterns.

Chihuahuas are very small and easy to care for, and they are also a very gentle and likeable breed.

Terriers such as this West Highland White like to keep active. So they may enjoy chasing squirrels in the park.

Terriers

These lively little dogs are bold by nature, because they were bred for hunting. Even today, terriers catch and kill rats very easily. Since they originally lived outside on farms, they often have wiry coats that protect them in bad weather. Most terrier breeds come from Great Britain. They like to dig in flowerbeds and can be short-tempered.

King Charles Spaniel

Some smaller breeds were created just as pets. A number of those that are bred today, such as the King Charles spaniel, first became popular in the royal courts of Europe hundreds of years ago.

King Charles spaniels were bred just to be pampered as pets.

Choosing your dog

There are many places where you can obtain a dog. If you want a puppy, then it is important to find a reliable breeder. You can ask your vet, or look in the advertisement columns of specialist dog magazines. Alternatively, you may want to contact your kennel club organization for advice. They can refer you to the breed society, where you can find breeders of the dog you want. Searching on the Internet with the help of an adult can help to find such people.

Kennel clubs and breeders can help you to find the dog you want.

Deciding on a breed

There are over 300 different breeds of dogs, which have been bred for many purposes – from guarding people to pulling sleds and herding sheep. It's important to find out as much as you can about a breed before making a choice. Otherwise, you may pick a dog that you like because of the way it looks, but which may be too active or not very friendly. It helps to visit dog shows, so that you can see the dogs and talk with their owners.

Rescued dogs

You can also look for a dog at one of the rescue societies, which have a variety of puppies and older dogs who need new homes. Beware of taking on an adult dog unless you are sure about its history. It may be bad-tempered and difficult to manage, and could possibly wreck furniture and household items.

Puppies are cute and should grow into great companions, but they need to be trained. A friendly, older dog that is used to living indoors with a family may be easier to manage.

Some dogs are less suitable as pets for children. Rottweilers, for example, are very strong, which means they can be difficult to control on a leash.

Choosing a puppy

When you are looking at a litter of puppies, it can be very hard to choose one, and this may tempt you to want two puppies. This would be expensive, however, and two puppies living together can be harder to train. Remember, too, that puppies grow into bigger dogs and need to have enough space.

Puppies usually stay with their mother until they are at least six weeks old.

Healthy puppies are lively when they are awake and are interested in everything that is going on around them.

Health matters

Ask when or if the puppies have had any vaccinations, and also when they were dewormed. Remember to get your new dog's vaccination certificate, so that you can have this updated by your vet when you need to. You should schedule a check-up for your new pet soon after you bring it home, to make sure that it is healthy.

Ask your vet how you can help keep your dog healthy and happy.

It is a good idea to bring your new dog home in a secure carrier or box.

The journey home

When taking your puppy home, you may want to travel with it on your lap, but the journey could upset your pet, causing it to struggle or possibly even be sick. It is best to place it in a special carrier or a sturdy cardboard box lined with old newspaper.

Your dog's home

Try to get everything ready for your dog ahead of time, so that you can settle your pet into its new home without delay. In the case of a puppy, you may want to get a special wire pen that clips together, where your pet can be safely housed at times. This will help to prevent the puppy from slipping out of your home when a door is open. You will need to be very careful, because puppies cannot be allowed out safely into public places such as parks until they have had their vaccinations. Also, they will not have any traffic sense and may run straight across a road even if there is a car coming.

Using a baby gate is a good way to keep your dogs in one part of the home.

Dogs like to run around outside in the fresh air. You can make your garden a safe place for them to play.

Keep your dog safe outdoors

Even with an older dog, you will need to check that the garden is secure, so that there is no risk of your new pet slipping out under a gate or a fence. Dogs can also jump very well, so if you have a low fence, you may need to make this higher in some way.

Why puppies chew

When a puppy starts to teethe, it is natural for it to start chewing. It is very important to give your pet chews at this stage, because they can help to relieve the pain of the new teeth coming through the gums. Chews can also prevent the puppy from damaging items around the home. Wait until the puppy is six months old before you buy it a new bed – the old one will be badly damaged by its teeth.

A dog likes to feel safe and snug in its own little bed.

Play is important

Puppies are more likely to be naughty if they are bored and feel left out, so it is very important that you play regularly with your pet. You should be able to find a wide range of toys at your local pet store. You can start training your puppy straight away too – it should soon learn to drop objects that it has been carrying in its mouth and sit down on command.

Playing with your dog is essential as it will stop it becoming bored and naughty.

Fetch

Your dog will want to join in any game. Throwing and catching are what dogs enjoy the best. Your dog will soon learn to bring items back to you in its mouth.

In a game of fetch, your dog will love bringing items back to you.

Danger!

Be very careful with electrical flexes at this stage, because if a puppy gnaws through the outer plastic cable with its teeth, then it could end up being electrocuted. Should you find your puppy chewing a flex, always turn off and disconnect the plug first, before doing anything else.

Make sure that you keep flexes like these out of reach from your dog.

You can sharpen a puppy's reflexes and train it to jump by gently throwing a ball for it to catch.

Feeding

Dogs, like their wolf ancestor, are omnivores. This means that they will eat both meat and vegetables, as well as fruit, although they usually prefer to eat meat when they are given a choice. If you prefer, though you can now buy some tasty vegetarian foods for your pet dog.

Dogs like to eat meaty canned food, but will also eat dried food.

Dog biscuits help to keep gums and teeth healthy.

No need to cook

Today, few people cook food specially for their dogs, since it is much easier to use prepared food that contains everything your dog should need to stay healthy. If you do give them home-cooked food, they will also need extra vitamins and minerals.

Be sure to give your dog the right amount of food.

Different dog foods

There are several types of dog food available from pet stores and supermarkets. The canned food looks most like meat, and once it is opened, needs to be stored in a refrigerator. Dogs often prefer this food, and it can also be mixed with dry food.

More owners are now using dry dog food for their pets, however, partly because it is easier to store. Dry food does not need to be kept chilled, but can simply be stored in a cupboard. Also, a pack of dry food provides a number of meals, whereas a can usually only contains one or two meals.

How much?

Be careful to follow the feeding instructions on the pack, so that you avoid giving your dog too much food. Otherwise, your pet will become overweight, and this can shorten its lifespan. If you cannot feel your dog's ribs, then it probably needs to go on a diet. Ask your vet for diet advice.

Mealtimes

Don't change the diet of a new puppy suddenly, because this can cause it to have a stomach upset. As your dog grows older, you can reduce the number of meals that your pet has each day, down to one or two, and change from puppy food to an adult diet. Always provide your pet's food in a heavy, earthenware bowl, which cannot be tipped over easily. Use the same type of bowl for drinking water, which needs to be provided fresh every day.

Chews help to clean a dog's teeth and can be used for training.

Early training

Mealtimes provide an ideal opportunity to start training a puppy. Before placing the food bowl on the floor, always persuade your puppy to sit. You may need to apply gentle pressure to the hindquarters at first, but puppies usually learn the command of "sit" very quickly. Do not tease your puppy if it does not behave as you want though, because this may make it become aggressive. After a meal, your puppy will want to relieve itself, so place it outside in the garden or take it for a walk, and encourage it with the command "be clean".

By telling your puppy to sit before giving it its food, you will quickly teach it to follow commands.

Bones and milk

There is no need to give your dog beef bones for its teeth. These are messy and can be harmful if they splinter. Chews are more commonly used for this purpose today, and they help to keep the teeth clean. Dogs do not need to drink milk, and some dogs may not even be able to digest it properly.

Grooming

Originally, poodles were clipped so that they could retrieve ducks.

Certain dogs need much more grooming than others – the immaculate clipped appearance of poodles, for example, is the result of lengthy grooming. Many people think this is just done for fashion, but it is a reflection of the breed's past. Poodles were first bred as retrievers that dived into water to bring back ducks that had been shot. The hair on their joints was trimmed, so they were able to swim more easily but did not become chilled in cold water. The pom-pom on their tail meant they could be seen easily. Today, this type of grooming is often done at a canine grooming salon, not by the dog's owner.

Coat care

You will certainly need a brush and comb so that you can prevent your dog's coat from developing mats. This is most likely to happen in the case of dogs that have long coats. Even though puppies of such breeds have much shorter hair at first, compared with adult dogs. However, it is still important to groom your pet regularly from an early age, so that it gets used to the brushing and doesn't wriggle about.

It is usually sufficient just to run the comb through the fur, in the same way that you comb your own hair, but when a dog is moulting it will probably need more brushing, so that the loose fur can be removed from the coat.

If you train your puppy to relax and enjoy the experience of being brushed, it will always let you groom its coat without a struggle.

Check for flea droppings, which are little black specks in the fur.

Bathing your dog

Every three months or so, a dog is likely to need a bath, to prevent it becoming too smelly. Choose a fine day and, with the help of an adult, wash your pet in an outdoor tub if possible. Partly fill this with tepid water, and then lift your dog in, gradually wetting its coat. You can use a special dog shampoo to clean its fur, then rinse this out thoroughly. Be sure that the shampoo does not get into your pet's eyes. Finally, wrap your dog in a towel and bring it indoors so it can dry off without getting chilled.

Flea alert

Always look out for fleas. The first clue may be that your dog scratches more often than usual and starts nibbling its skin. You are more likely to recognize flea dirt, which appears as blackish specks in the fur, rather than the fleas themselves.

Groom your pet outside if you suspect that it has fleas. Any fleas that jump off outdoors are less likely to reinfest your dog or to bite you. Flea bites on people are red and very itchy, but fleas won't live on our bodies. The fleas can be spread between cats and dogs though, so both pets in a home need to be treated with special flea powder or similar treatment if one has fleas. You'll also need to wash your pet's bedding, or replace it, and vacuum to remove any young fleas that may be there.

1 Rub a little bit of the dog shampoo into the fur, then rinse it off well.

2 Dry your dog with a big, fluffy towel – be careful when you dry its face.

3 If it is cold outside, let the dog stay in a warm room until it is completely dry, so that it doesn't catch a chill.

Dogs outdoors

It is important to start training your puppy from an early stage, so that it will walk properly, without pulling on a lead. The first step will be to obtain a collar. This should have sufficient holes so that it can be let out as your puppy's neck grows.

Do not worry if your pet tries to wriggle out of its collar at first. It will soon become used to wearing it. You should also put an identity tag on the collar, which gives the dog's name and your telephone number. This means that if your puppy strays or gets lost, anyone who finds your pet can get in touch with you quickly. You can also include the vet's phone number.

A check or choke chain can help to stop your dog pulling.

This type of collar must be fitted carefully – ask an adult to help if you are unsure.

To start with, keep your puppy a short distance from you on the lead.

Leads

Extendible leads are ideal for training purposes – at first they can be kept quite short, so that your puppy will walk alongside you, but you can let them out later. Always keep your pet on the same side of you, because you could easily trip if the dog darts under your feet. Also, try to walk with your puppy alongside a fence or wall, since this will make it harder for your pet to pull away from you. Pause occasionally and instruct your puppy to sit, as this will be necessary when you are waiting to cross a road.

Persevere with training until your puppy obeys your commands.

Further training

You will need some help from an adult to train your puppy well, and you may want to go with your dog to special training classes. These are usually fun, and they help your dog to meet other dogs and become friends with them.

Once your puppy has made good progress, you can take it out with an adult to a safe area. At first, puppies get excited and often don't behave well when they are outdoors, so be patient with your pet. In safe areas away from traffic, let out the lead a bit further, which will let your puppy have a run. Always call the dog back to you, and reward it with a piece of carrot, so that hopefully, once your pet is ready to be let off the lead outdoors, it will return as soon as it is called. There are even special dog whistles that you can buy for this purpose.

Reward your dog for behaving well by giving it sticks of carrot.

Journeys with your dog

Whenever you travel with your pet in a car, it is a good idea to use a safety crate, or a dog guard to keep it behind the seats. This will stop your dog from interfering with the driver, which could cause an accident.

A dog guard will stop your pet from leaning or jumping out of a car window.

Away on holiday

Depending on where you are going for your holiday, it may be possible to take your dog with you – although if you leave the country, you may need special veterinary treatment and documents, so find out well in advance. If you're not going abroad, you may be able to find hotels that welcome dogs, although it is not fair to take your dog with you and then leave it in the hotel room. Many people book their dog into a boarding kennel while they are away, where their pet will have the company of people, as well as other dogs.

Don't be worried about leaving your dog as you can find a good boarding kennel for it to stay in.

Remember to bring your dog's bed, food and toys on holiday.

Reserving a kennel space

Book your dog into a kennel as early as possible – they usually get very busy at holiday times, and you may have trouble finding a space for your pet. If you haven't used the kennel before, it is a good idea to visit first, to be sure that your dog will be happy there while you are away. All good kennels will want to see your dog's vaccination certificate. You may want to have your dog vaccinated against kennel cough too.

Travels with your dog

Always remember to take a water bottle and bowl, so that when you stop on your journey you can give your dog a drink. Rinse the water bottle out thoroughly each night, and then refill it with fresh water in the morning.

Fit and healthy

Dogs rarely get ill, but you will need to deworm your pet regularly. Your vet will be able to provide advice on this, and give you the necessary medication. It can be difficult giving tablets or pills to dogs, although you may be able to hide the wormer in some meaty canned food. Hopefully, your dog will swallow the tablet without realizing it. Even so, puppies should be accustomed to having their mouths opened from an early age, so that you can give a tablet easily if you need to. Drop it to the back of the dog's mouth, then hold the jaws closed until the dog swallows.

It is a good idea to train your dog to let you open its mouth, so that you can give it pills when you need to.

Dental care

Being able to open its mouth will also mean that you can check your dog's teeth without fear of being bitten. Regular brushing once a week or so with a special dog toothpaste and brush should help to prevent dental problems, such as inflamed gums.

As your dog gets older, you will need to look out for early signs of illnesses such as kidney problems, heart disease and arthritis. Ask your vet if you are worried about any unusual symptoms.

Old age

Health problems are more likely to occur as your dog gets older. Its breath may start to smell unpleasant, and although this is often a sign of bad teeth, it can also be linked with kidney problems. It is a good idea to have your pet's health checked every six months or so by your vet as it becomes older, so that any problems can be detected and can then be treated at an early stage.

This edition is published by Armadillo, an imprint of Anness Publishing Ltd,
Blaby Road, Wigston, Leicestershire LE18 4SE; info@anness.com

www.annesspublishing.com

If you like the images in this book and would like to investigate using them for publishing, promotions
or advertising, please visit our website www.practicalpictures.com for more information.

© Anness Publishing Ltd 2012

All rights reserved. No part of this publication may be reproduced, stored in a retrieval system, or
transmitted in any way or by any means, electronic, mechanical, photocopying, recording or otherwise,
without the prior written permission of the copyright holder.

A CIP catalogue record for this book is available from the British Library.

Publisher: Joanna Lorenz
Managing Editor: Linda Fraser
Editor: Sarah Uttridge
Designer: Linda Penny
Photographer: Paul Bricknell
Production Controller: Pirong Wang

The publishers would like to thank Rosie Anness, Grace Crissell, Connor Johnson and
Catherine McGovern for appearing in this book. With special thanks to Len Anness,
Ju Gosling and Janet Johnson for providing the dogs.

PUBLISHER'S NOTE
Although the advice and information in this book are believed to be accurate and true at the time of going
to press, neither the authors nor the publisher can accept any legal responsibility or liability for any errors
or omissions that may have been made nor for any inaccuracies nor for any loss, harm or injury that
comes about from following instructions or advice in this book.

Manufacturer: Anness Publishing Ltd, Blaby Road, Wigston, Leicestershire LE18 4SE, England
For Product Tracking go to: www.annesspublishing.com/tracking
Batch: 2925-21994-1127